The Bell-Branch Rings

Books by Dorsha Hayes

THE AMERICAN PRIMER

CHICAGO: CROSSROADS OF ENTERPRISE

MRS. HEATON'S DAUGHTER

WHO WALK WITH THE EARTH

THE BELL-BRANCH RINGS

The
Bell-Branch Rings

Selected Poems by
Dorsha Hayes

William · L · Bauhan · Publisher
Dublin · New Hampshire
1972

Copyright © 1972 by Dorsha Hayes
All Rights Reserved. No portion of this book may be reproduced without permission of the publisher.
Library of Congress Catalog Card No. 72-85141
ISBN: 87233-028-1

The author extends her thanks to the editors of THE LYRIC, POET LORE, THE LITERARY REVIEW, THE CHRISTIAN SCIENCE MONITOR, BITTERROOT, SCIMITAR AND SONG, CHALLENGE, THE COOPERATOR, IMPRINTS QUARTERLY, QUADRANT, PSYCHOLOGICAL PERSPECTIVES—The Bulletin of the Analytical Psychology Club of New York, THE DIAMOND ANTHOLOGY, and THE INTERNATIONAL WHO'S WHO IN POETRY ANTHOLOGY, for permission to include here poems which have appeared in their publications.

Cover design by Marian Bowes

COMPOSED AND PRINTED AT
THE CABINET PRESS, INC., MILFORD, N. H.

To the memory of Paul Hayes

Contents

PART ONE

The Bell-Branch	11
Resurgence	12
Ballade in Lament for Eloquence	13
Orpheus	14
Of Lasting Things	15
Farmland, Seen from a Train	16
Loss	17
The Unredeemed	18
Outside of Eden	19
Call It a Prayer	20
To a Jungian Analyst	21
Nightmare	22
I See Her Plain	24
In Memoriam for the Analyst	25
Fire Hazard	26
Without a Look Askance	27
I Remember Ben	28
Pursued, Pursuer	29
Rave, Rage, O Rebel	30
Darwinian Concept	31
Words for Singing	32
Old Tom	33

PART TWO

Reverie	37
There's No Potion to Be Had	38
And Have You Now No Thought of Me?	39
Waiting	40
At Parting	41
Then Let Me Soar	42
To a Friend Who Counsels Caution	43

With No Tomorrow	44
Confession	45
The Harp Longs for the Player	46
Love-Sight	47
To My Lover, Growing Old	48

PART THREE

The Knowing	51
Variation on a Villanelle by Dylan Thomas	52
As in a Dream, I Wait	53
No Man Will Mourn	54
Let Love Rage	55
Not Body-Bound	56
Mind Flight in Sea Thirst	57
At Night, Alone	58
A Sudden Silence	59
The Symbol X	60
In a Dark Hour	61
The River	62
Monad	63
Rose	64
A Change in Weather	65
Until the Day of Ragnarok	66

PART FOUR

On Returning from the Metropolitan Museum	69
Ballade for the Lost Poetry of Dance	70
The Dance is a Flash in Time	71
With Dancing Feet	72
To a Poet Who Belittles Rhyme and Rhythm	73
Words Are for Sharing	74
The Villanelle	75
A Useful Beast	76
"O Sweet Everlasting Voices—"	77
For Kindness Shown	78

Part I

THE BELL-BRANCH

They came, times past, into a forest glade
or an assembly in a banquet hall,
a green branch borne, and on each branch, arrayed,
were little silver bells that gave the call
to poetry that would be given out.
Such was the custom in old Druid times
when poets sought through song to bring about
an easeful pleasure with their chanted rhymes.
Now, lacking audience and branch and bell,
I still would seek with woven words to bring
again some semblance of that ancient spell,
drawn out of heart's deep-stored remembering.

RESURGENCE

It comes, it comes! Oh, let it come!
— the cadenced, inborn surge,
upthrusting outflow from the man,
man rhythmical, oh, rhythmical
as heart-beat, earth-spin, tide-pull,
man, wisdom-stored, dream-stuffed,
singer down centuries of must-be-melody,
heart-need, grief-cry, soul-hope,
shared, shared, insearch, outreach,
the man-shaped, form-found song—
Oh, bless the coming out from chaos!

BALLADE IN LAMENT FOR ELOQUENCE

The dazed fixated look in lovers' eyes,
magnetic mingle in a sudden bind,
the two now fused and handfast in surprise
at being struck by sky-fire and entwined.
All utterance inept and left behind,
they talk with tender touch and blending kiss,
and every look outraces fumbled mind—
Where is the eloquence to speak of this?

And what if suddenly without surmise
of severance, death strikes, and now the grind
of grief is known to one whose love decries
catastrophe's acceptance, raging, blind,
without capacity to be resigned,
plunged downward, wailing, to the black abyss,
lost utterly to light, in grief confined—
Where is the eloquence to speak of this?

And what of one to whom the soul supplies
a sustenance so rare and of a kind
that in a sudden splendor glorifies
the being to a height where God, divined
in ecstasy, will leave a man enshrined
in love's supernal strength and lasting bliss,
without a fret which way his road will wind—
Where is the eloquence to speak of this?

Envoy

Dear Man! So much you've felt, for much you've pined,
and all our speech is shambling artifice!
Your fate with love or grief or God aligned—
Where is the eloquence to speak of this?

ORPHEUS

Your head torn off and dripping red still sang
and sang, for so the story spread,
when tossed into a stream, sun-silvered,
veined with purple as you bled.
Song trailing from pale parted lips
and pulsing throat, your fair head afloat
upon the winding, shining rivulet swirled on
past grassy fields a breeze had liquefied,
past rockstrewn hills aquiver in the sun,
through glades where leaf-made patterns swayed,
and still all those who thought you dead
could hear sweet singing from the severed head.

Though we may rave and run through rubble-rubbish
of our fallen towers in dread of powers
we have produced, the holocausts that could be loosed,
what wrong can shut the mouth of song?

OF LASTING THINGS

I mean to sing of lasting things
   for love of man who stands unbowed
     in all the turmoil of today,
   who is himself within a crowd
     and knows there is a single way
that he must go. Such knowing brings

a sanity inspiring love
   to make me sing of what endures
     within this man and can be found.
   No milling of the mob obscures
     his vision when his voice is drowned
and all he once had knowledge of

seems lost. Then may my songs make sense
   to tell of joy and sorrow known,
     of dreams, taut loyalties, and hope,
   recalling how a man alone
     can find it lies within his scope
to shape his own experience.

FARMLAND, SEEN FROM A TRAIN

See, see! Look now, swift passing—
Gain from governed land,
governed, measured, squared, prepared,
repeat, repeat, square by square,
green by green by gold by blond,
field by field on roll of hill and hollow dip
and over over where horizon wheels,
all in ripple roll of walking wind
in summer sun in harvest hope
of man's contriving—
Grow, grow, row on row, by plan, by prayer,
by earth, by air, crop surviving!
   Now what can trouble the heart of man
   when earth will take and earth will give
   and man can make what he needs to live?
   Oh, what can trouble the heart of man!

LOSS

Why did I turn, quite suddenly,
expectant I would see
a tall white figure standing
where no human shape could be?
I turned ... saw nothing there.
But did a presence melt in air,
I, blinded in a flash
by rationality?

THE UNREDEEMED

On a dark day in a dripping wood
I met a tattered, weeping child
who wandered, wild, alone and lost,
so frail and pale, a specter
wind had lifted from a tomb.
   What ails you, Child?
Affrighted, fugitive, a moan,
she fluttered back from where I stood
as though a wind had blown.
   Child, speak. What doom can bring
   you to this darkened wood?
She beat her hands and quickened in retreat.
   I am a wicked thing, and yours, she said,
and turned and fled and faded in the gloom.

OUTSIDE OF EDEN

To seek an absolute to which I'd bind
belief, and loyal, resolute, defend,
to test each truth in hope it would transcend
all doubt, and that this twisting of the mind
led here and there in hope to find
an absolute that it could comprehend,
that it could celebrate, so call an end
to search, the meaning found, divined—

Oh no! I'll not have answers when I die!
Far better watch a snail ooze on its way,
and all small things that, governed, follow rules.
Let be, be still, abandon all the schools
of rigid thought, and in a dream obey
what life alone can teach that will apply.

CALL IT A PRAYER

Oh, shatter my self-image, God!
Take me apart, let me disintegrate,
re-form, be in no fixed and final pattern set!
Eradicate conceptions of the mind
that bind, bend, break, mistake
direction of the living latency!
Pulled out of every doubt
and all complacency, the questing beast
made holy-natural, released to live
twice-born and unbetrayed,
shaped to your shaping I would come
to some semblance in your image made.

TO A JUNGIAN ANALYST

This woman with the frowning brows of thought,
so sternly kind, deals with the blind, the caught
despairing fugitive who yet has trust
that somehow in the labyrinth of 'must'
   and 'will,' the ego-lash of pain, a way
exists. She makes a consecrated place
for stricken, haunted souls, strayed from the race
of men and longing to return. God's hound
she is, upon the unrelenting round
   that makes the night transparent as the day,
that searches every gully, every dive,
in which the soul may yet be half alive.
What waves of sorrow break about her feet!
What shoddy of evasion and deceit!
   What ghosts take shape, what devils fill the room!
A mater dolorosa, wise, serene,
skilled doctor of her art, she waits the clean
acceptance of the truth, the seeking soul
released, set free, at last made whole,
   and no more backward looking to the womb.

NIGHTMARE

Hurrying, hurrying, all guilty ones must—
I? No. Why?
Where—? I go in.
Cavern. Dark. Vast. Gloom. Wind.
No sun shines here. It never shone in here.
Trapped wind. Cold. Vapors.
Night's hiding place. Mole's house.
Shapes—there are Shapes. Women.
Wind-stirred Shapes, scattered in gloom,
watching, waiting. For—?
Hurrying, hurrying, a downward slope to—
My mother. Thin, white, prostrate on a bier.
A finger points: a scrap of paper on her chest,
my name, the words addressed to me:
I shall live only as long as your lips press mine.
A whirl of wind. The Watchers drift closer,
mole-silent, owl-eyed, waiting. Evil.
"I came as quickly as I could."
Do they hear? Will they believe?
The kiss commanded: I bend and press chill lips.
The thin lips twitch, a tic that gives
a biting motion to the jaws.
You have neglected me.
Did she say it? Was it heard?
They know. They will believe.
"I came as quickly . . ."
Lips twitch. Jaws munch. Cold air fans my cheek.
The Shapes draw close.

Yellow eyes, round, bright as owl or cat
gleam out of darkness in a ring.
My mother dying, and I—
"I came!"
Loud, protesting. Will they not hear?
I bend again to give the kiss demanded.
Lips part, mouth opens, opens wide, cavernous.
She means to bite—
GHOUL, GHOUL, DEVOURING GHOUL!
I am shaking in the cold wind
that blows from Nowhere.
Who is screaming, screaming?
Stop stop stop stop stop

I SEE HER PLAIN

What if my youth was mangled,
long years lost to find the kind
of being I so longed to be?
What if I wake half strangled
by the hag of nightmare,
sweating cold because of old
remembered misery?
I now stand free and see her plain
and know my debt, for she was pitiful.

Let this be said, and said with love:
I can recall when she was beautiful,
so blithely gay and filled with grace
I'd stop my play to run to her
and find my heaven in embrace.

IN MEMORIAM FOR THE ANALYST

O Lady lying low, can we now mourn
when memory beyond all writing on a tomb
goes back into that room, that *temenos*
you built where guilt and dread
of troubled mind could find release,
could know the touch of peace,
a torment turned to purpose and a chaos shaped,
where, with your aid, the helping word,
the dumb, made unafraid, could speak,
the netted bird of spirit freed?
A room, a lady in it,
and a world re-lit.
How can we mourn a fate fulfilled?

FIRE HAZARD

Filled with a clutter of unsorted stuff
a spark can set a man ablaze. What's there
heaped high among stored rubbish at a puff
will burst in flame. No man can be aware
of how inflammable he is, how prone
to what can rage beyond control, unless
the piled up litter of his life is known
to him, and he is able to assess
what hazard he is in, what could ignite.
A man, disordered and undisciplined,
lives in the peril of a panic flight
before the onrush of a flaming wind.
  Does it now seem I seek to be profound?
  I stand on smoking ash and blackened ground.

WITHOUT A LOOK ASKANCE

God save us when we're masked
   by either circumstance
or choice! Not having asked
   for human tolerance,
caught cruelly in pride,
   each one of us believes
that he alone must hide
   defect, and so deceives
himself. But when we dare
   to know we're lame or bent,
and this is no way rare,
   why, we can give assent
to what we are, and see,
   without a look askance,
how well, how merrily,
   the loving cripples dance.

I REMEMBER BEN

No one would call him coward though he fled
   from what he could not face.
      While others, fleeing, sank in mud,
   he soared in windy space,
clutched at the stars, and dangling overhead,
      sang how, above the blood
dominion, spirit loosed in fantasy
   could make a shining world
      for gentle, child-like souls such as his own.
   Wind-swung, star-crazed, he whirled,
and fashioned out of anguish, ecstasy,
      not for himself alone;
so needful of a love, he gave it out
   to every child he knew;
      they followed him as he went up and down . . .
   Ah Ben, folks speak of you,
remembered now as simple and devout,
      but mostly as Pied Piper in the town.

PURSUED, PURSUER

There is no refuge for the man
   in flight from self, but who can say
      when flight is not pursuit? What sent
   poor Thompson on his hounded way?
   There seems to be an innate plan
     of human growth and measurement

of what a man would wish to be.
   Conformity can make us ill;
      we are not made to be one size,
   one shape, but with a God-sent skill
attempt to find a sanctity
     within ourselves that we can prize.

What urges on the running man?
   Pursued, pursuer—who can tell?
     For some will run in cowardice
   to an unquestionable hell,
but there are also those who ran
   and came at last to Paradise.

RAVE, RAGE, O REBEL

Your love-bred bitterness breaks out
defending excellent intent
from petty pulling down, smug quibble,
and the shrug, the turn away.
How could you be content, O Rebel,
to take opinion from the crowd,
their thumbs turned down to signify
all dreams are worthless, let them die?
Oh yes, yes, you could be kind
to their unpitiful pretense
if you could drug the mind, deny
the loyalty, the leap of love
to what must soar to live.
Why, holy is your anger, your attack,
your backing of belief! Rave, rage,
O Rebel, say your say and stand like Swift
within the flaming fury of your love!

DARWINIAN CONCEPT

There's only one of me upon this earth,
in all the myriads, no duplicate.
I am, that never was, nor will be.
Compounded, good and bad,
conditioned, chance and choice,
I must be me without conformity
to cult or creed.

Imposed responsibility!
For what am I but Nature's try
with different molds
for what might be?

WORDS FOR SINGING

In defeat or in renown,
thorn or laurel, wear your crown.
Fate's a fool who plays the clown!

When a man is struck a blow,
who can say what way he'll go?
Some will rise, some sink below.

Man's response will shape his fate.
He will come to love or hate,
learn a lot, or learn too late.

Thorn or laurel, wear your crown.
Do we know who's up, who's down?
Fate's a fool who plays the clown!

OLD TOM

Fur faded to pale yellow without gloss,
ears fringed as battle flags, most honorable
insignia of courtship claims defended,
all territorial rights maintained,
you slithered through the held screened door,
accepting custom, yet regally deliberate.
Outside, you paused, blinking at brightness,
and then set out quite warily
upon a way so often trod.
A yard's length from the door
you stopped to test the scent,
small upward jerks of head,
a curved forepaw upheld.
A single swish of tail and on you went,
slow moving patch of yellow on cropped green,
and coming to the rock-pile wall,
no longer bunching for the spring,
you crawled from stone to stone,
came to the top and paused again,
reflective, dubious. Another lash of tail—
defiance? resolution?—and you began
the vanishing descent into the woods.

I called that night, I called the next,
I went on calling, searching, for a week.

O Queenly Bast, Great Bast of Egypt,
Serene Protector of the Many-lived,
did you lead a little aged cat
to sun-dried laurel leaves deep in the wood
where he lay down, curled into sleep,
and never woke to know he could no longer
leap or love or lick a wound with pride?

Part II

REVERIE

I did not bring this thing about,
no, not by any hope or scheme,
yet it has come to me.
And shall I turn it out, disown the dream,
take counsel with myself of coming grief
because the sweetness of this love
—beyond belief!—cannot be mine?
Oh, love is life at summit height!
What can I be but tender with delight
and thankful it has come to me?

THERE'S NO POTION TO BE HAD

Our lips have never met and never shall,
though when eyes meet they cannot turn away.
Fixed fast by love, we gaze and stare, dumb, dazed,
and no word comes.

And will not come. What is there we could say
whose lips have never met and never shall?
Eye-talk is all we have of love, struck, snared,
and no word comes.

And cannot come. We have not Iseult's drink
to drug the mind! We two cannot forget
our lips have never met and never shall,
and no word comes.

Dumb, dazed, and stricken, snared, we know, we know,
and knowing, still we stare, and every look
is union, binding, blinding, taut and true,
though lips have never met and never shall.

AND HAVE YOU NOW NO THOUGHT OF ME?

Well, let it be! I shall not ask
who never asked to have the gift
you gave to me. Should I then task
you now with telling why the rift
has come? What use is there to gloss
with words what lies outside of sense?
I'll seek some gain within the loss
and call what was 'experience.'

Love shudders at the words I say.
What can be said, you gone away?

WAITING

Tomorrow I shall rise and dress
as nicely as I can,
a woman, waiting for a man,
and I shall sit precisely,
quite sedate,
and I shall tell myself:
It's not too late!
And yet I know you will not come,
though I shall wait.

AT PARTING

Can we not part, my dear, without reproach?
Keep tenderness alive in thinking back,
not let the bleeding bitterness encroach,
no cruelty to specify what lack
was in us, you or me, that love has died?
Recall love's coming, how we did not choose
yet relished all that love supplied,
a gift that only ingrates, when they lose,
would cease to value. Stay in love with love
if not with me, and seek to cherish, keep,
as I shall try, what's worth the dreaming of.
Let some small sadness come before you sleep,
but come in gentleness for love's own sake
that love may rise again, and life re-make.

THEN LET ME SOAR

What taint could come upon our love
worse than denial of it?
A wing-clipped bird grows wild
in its restraint! What trial is this
you put on me that I, earth-bound,
must hop and flop along the ground
when I could soar to any height?
O Keeper of my Love, let me take wing
and I will bring you quarry from the sky
and you will sing in your delight
to see me rise to air-romp, revelling,
wind-riding, high-gliding, dart-diving,
subsiding in a flutter at your feet!

TO A FRIEND WHO COUNSELS CAUTION

Then call me fool! Oh yes, I know I am.
But tell me, did you ever love a man
with love so wild, so sweet, it seemed that Pan
himself had piped you to his bed? What sham
can I assume, lost in the dithyramb
of love and magicked far beyond the ban
of sense? My love called to me, and I ran.
Impetuous, you say? Who gives a damn!

I shall be singing praise of love's misrule!
Why yes, we thought of witches, warlocks, once,
believed possessions could be fixed by spells.
Dear friend, above all magic, love excels!
Though I'm bewitched and simple as a dunce,
it does no good for you to call me fool!

WITH NO TOMORROW

I love you now, today,
with no tomorrow.
How can I say
our love will last?
I have known love that bloomed
and passed, death-doomed
or fading like a flower.
I shall not borrow sorrow
asking what an hour may bring!
Love is the salve we have to give
who live through loss to learn
not then or when but now
is all we have.

CONFESSION

I have been cruel, meaning to be kind.
With warning words, denial of love's bind,
I sought to sever, hoping you would find
me all unworthy, dear, and take love light.

The snare from which I hoped to set you free
has sprung; well set by love, it snaps on me,
and I who do deserve your cruelty
am caught by kindness, and your true love's might.

THE HARP LONGS FOR THE PLAYER

O Harper, loose the song!
   My strings are tuned and taut
but mute. I do so long
   to be caressed, distraught,
made vibrant at your touch!
   You only can console,
give solace to so much
   that you alone control.
Oh, do not be afraid
   to stroke the aching strings
lest, in a quick cascade
   of feeling freed, heart sings
in riot, reason lost!
   Why should not you and I
be joined and tumult tossed
   though we both laugh and cry?

LOVE-SIGHT

Love blind? Oh no, it gives us sight!
  Why, I have seen the morning star
so luminous in early light
    it hung in heaven like a moon
    new-born. I've seen at summer noon
  a hawk slide in a spiral far
into the blaze, no beat of wing
  in that slow soaring spin. I've seen
day end in glory, burnishing
    a hallelujah sunset sky
    aflame and streaming, zenith high,
  and all the west incarnadine.
Love gave me eyes to stand and gaze
  as though I had not seen before,
and all I look upon, I praise,
    turned innocent in my delight
    and filled with wonder at the sight
  of all that once I would ignore.

TO MY LOVER, GROWING OLD

Drowse, dear, in that big chair of yours,
half dozing, dream of me,
wrapped warmly in my love
with no anxiety. For I will come
when come I can, and lie within your arms
and know content to match the dream
you dream, half dozing in your chair.

Part III

THE KNOWING

No, not by gazing at a human skull
and musing, Hamlet-wise, death will annul
a Caesar or the fairest who drew breath,
no, not by any somber thought of death
will the full horror of the knowing come.
But lovers in the spent delirium
of passion sated, lying locked, warm flesh
on flesh, so bound together in love's mesh
there is no thought but only body-joy
in after-ease of love, if then a flash
of knowing came to one—Death will destroy
what now I hold so close, change all to ash,
grey ash grown cold and heap of blackened bone—
Still lying locked, that lover lies alone.

VARIATION ON A VILLANELLE BY DYLAN THOMAS

No, do not rage, beloved. Go in peace.
   The dying of the light must come to all.
Let rage and grief be mine, and yours, release.

Cannot this frantic, futile struggle cease?
   What man who fights with death can win the brawl?
No, do not rage, beloved. Go in peace.

How could I bear your agony's increase?
   Dream deep, and into dreaming gently fall.
Let rage and grief be mine, and yours, release.

Let go of life, let go of your long lease!
   Why should the end of suffering appall?
No, do not rage, beloved. Go in peace.

There must be angel song, some Cantatrice
   to ease your way in answering the Call!
Let rage and grief be mine, and yours, release.

Sleep, sleep, my love, and know a sweet surcease.
   Before Lord Death all men are mortal small.
No, do not rage, beloved. Go in peace.
Let rage and grief be mine, and yours, release.

AS IN A DREAM, I WAIT

I stand in dark beside the door
at midnight and I call to you
to come. Tales told in all old lore
of how the dead will rise are true—
I know they are! The house is still;
come now and I alone will know.
Oh, take whatever shape you will
or none but by some evanescent flow
inform me, make your presence known!
If that dog on the hill would howl,
or wind would lift, the air would moan,
if I could hear the hooting owl,
or where you've stepped a floor board creak—
some sound old folks have said they hear
when dear ones come who cannot speak
and yet would signal they are near.
You died three days ago. It's true.
But all last night, the night before,
my love, I've sought to summon you,
and still I'm standing by the door.

NO MAN WILL MOURN

No man will mourn me when I die,
she said, and grieved because of this.
Oh Lady, Lady, there is bliss
in knowing not my man but I
now mourn! I am the legatee
of loss and know the grip of grief.
You cannot guess with what relief
I say my man won't mourn for me!

LET LOVE RAGE

Dear heart, I saw the moon tonight, and thought
three moons have come to full since you have died.
Intent in struggle to be fortified
I have seen none. This sudden sight has brought
my sorrow to the full, and now, distraught,
salt tears have come and I am one with tide
the moon can pull. How could my grief subside,
unfaced, and by a coward dread held taut?

Now let love rage for you gone from my reach.
Not once again beside the tide-torn sea
in its eternal sway shall you and I
stand joined to watch Night's Queen ride up the sky.
Why, I am stranded in neap tide's debris,
a flapping fish that gasps upon the beach!

NOT BODY-BOUND

Where are you now, my love,
who was so live so little while ago?
Do I only, flesh-meshed, long, alone?
Or you, could you be near, know, need, share longing
for the jump-quick, heart-jibe joining
we two knew?
But how, your body gone to ground,
can you not be
who were not body-bound in life?
In streaming, dreaming, spaceless, speculative search,
you, essential you, oh, spirit-sparked, skimmed free
of flesh-bind, thought sought, wrought, word-wrestled,
a mindscape made, wrung to a flow outsent—
All this, real, incorporeal, wave on wave—
Can this lie quiet in a grave?

MIND FLIGHT IN SEA THIRST

In stormy gusts a winter rain
drums and smacks my window pane,
and I, so dry, so city-sickened,
fly in mind to a deserted shore
low-levelled by the sea wind's sweep—
Wind-angered ocean in its leap and boom
assaults the tufted dunes,
clumped grey grasses waving, holding fast.
Sky aflow and billowing, torn, tumbled clouds,
dark as bruise on flesh, scud overhead.
Three sea birds on long slender wings
slide up the wind, careen, flash white
caught in a sudden spear of light,
their creaking cry a mockery of storm.
And I stand braced, astraddle, arms flung out,
and take, for my soul's sake,
wind-lash, rain-pelt, spray-sting,
made one with elemental energy—
in this wild flight of mind,
rain drumming on the pane.

AT NIGHT, ALONE

But love's affect we cannot lose. Its grace
remains, for we are altered when it comes,
a change then made that nothing can efface,
and though the thrust of grief benumbs
the heart, love's transformation will remain.
More woman now than I could be before,
despite the cost, I shall not lose the gain.
I have been loved; can I that love deplore?
And if I weep, and weeping turns to rage,
I do no honor to the one who died.
The living love within must now assuage
that grief by which we can be dignified.
   Dear heart, forgive me if I still do weep
   at night, alone, before I fall asleep.

A SUDDEN SILENCE

A sudden silence settles,
spreads, shifts, and settles.
The filled void holds.

A god has neared.

O little holy hollow
of unmoving time,
hold me, hold me.

Breath alters,
slow, deep, sea-rhythm.
Drink, drink rose-scented air.

Joy mounting, undulant,
surf-strong, wave on wave
of thrust and surge.

Hold me, hold me,
do not pass.
Let me hold fast.

In this stopped stillness
nothing moves and all is motion.
O holy hush of happiness ...

A god has neared.

THE SYMBOL X

I set down X, unknown, as symbol for my God.
It is a cross with two prongs based on earth,
two pointing to the sky, and it must do;
I make no claim to knowing more than I can know.
Say, then, I have no name, no image of my God,
but do not say I doubt that He is there.
A force, emergent, rare, not of my making,
can so thrill the swelling fullness of my heart
I shake with love, exultant and complete.
So, for the sake of miracle, I set down X.
It's said a man is made in likeness of his God;
if I can keep both feet upon the earth,
both arms uplifted to the sky,
at least I take my symbol's shape.
O my Sweet Lord, I try!

IN A DARK HOUR

What need for hope if heroism lives,
and if none such exists, what hope for man?
It's plain that we are blinded fugitives
from fate. Why, no man living forms a plan
but that some fling of fortune, unforeseen,
can hurl disaster on his best intent
and leave him weeping for what might have been.
What use to cry "unjust" or to lament?
Who promised justice that we can complain?
What dream confused us, led us to believe
that we had grown beyond the clutch of pain,
could live in joyful ease and never grieve,
evade catastrophe, untouched by fear?
Man's heritage is one of famine, flood,
of war, and plague, age-long in his career,
betrayal, man by man in baths of blood.
Do we not know what courage was required
through centuries in struggle to survive
and to what heights man's spirit has aspired
with all hope gone, but spirit still alive?

THE RIVER

Love will endure, the lover sighed,
there never was true love that died!
(The river raced in full spring tide.)

The sinner vowed, I will repent,
turn back the days I have misspent!
(The river rushed in its descent.)

The mourner wept beside the grave
and moaned, Each memory I'll save!
(The river met the ocean's wave.)

MONAD

Within the crowding pack we know the gross
communion of the beast, the fevered loin,
the jostle, the attack. Though we lie close
in love, we lie alone; flesh does not join.
Alone we come to life, alone we leave.
We can both give and get, possess a friend,
take pleasure in what work we can achieve,
yet we are separate from start to end.
A man must stand alone to be a man,
hold colloquy of self with Self, and seek,
among his devils and his gods, critique
of what he is, and how, within his span
of time before libido's lost or spent,
to find within himself what's permanent.

ROSE

Cat's claws on your long stem
repulse profanity of clumsy clutch,
small scimitars that guard your growth
from bud through bloom,
draw blood in your defense
that you may be inviolate,
petal on petal, overlapped and underlaid,
hiding the central mystery of seed
shown only as you die, and dying,
give your promise of perpetuance.

A CHANGE IN WEATHER

Now when my spirit stalks in gloom
   I tell myself a change is due;
this much at least I can assume.

I am of nature—there's the clue,
   and like the weather, I must change.
I cannot say what will ensue

but would it not indeed be strange
   if only I remained the same
in all of nature's shifting range?

I could, it's true, advance the claim
   that I and weather are not one,
remind myself of Will and Aim—

With all such sophistry be done!
Old Heraclitus knew the run—
It storms today?—tomorrow, sun.

UNTIL THE DAY OF RAGNAROK

Dream-maker, Soul-shaker,
bread am I and you the Baker!
Sift and knead and light the fire,
I shall rise to your desire
through the working of the yeast
that you give unto the least,
and will give, till in a pyre
all consuming, all expire,
and Man is no more partaker
of your stirring, O my Maker!

Part IV

ON RETURNING FROM THE METROPOLITAN MUSEUM

A man can make a lovely lasting thing,
container of a moment's mood now set
in permanence. A moment lived can bring
such solvent sweetness, spirit-true, beget
a flowering like a May in bloom, a gain,
a gift he longs to lift outside of time.
Through loving, labored skill, he will retain
in media of stone or paint or rhyme
what has been given, known; it will endure
to celebrate and to proclaim. Man's way;
no other sentient creature can secure
what time will whip away, or can repay
the gift from life. It lies within our norm
to brood on beauty, and to give it form.

BALLADE FOR THE LOST POETRY OF DANCE

The fact is there in history
and that is all. We know her name,
her art is now a mystery.
Yet Taglioni once became
renowned, enjoyed the highest fame.
Is there not reason for despair,
her poems lost beyond reclaim?
Only the dancer writes on air.

The poetry of dance can be
the sort fine words would only maim.
Indeed it has a subtlety,
a nuance, substance, in a frame
well wrought and styled that would not shame
the poet. But, of earthenware,
the body tires, it will go lame.
Only the dancer writes on air.

Fonteyn! Why, every devotee
rejoiced when she was made a Dame!
But dancers reach an apogee
and pass. Success? The telling's tame
when dancer dies. It is the same
for all within that field; their flare
goes out. It is a losing game.
Only the dancer writes on air.

Envoy

Dancer, set our hearts aflame!
Your passing moment's precious, rare!
No fault is yours, your art's to blame.
Only the dancer writes on air.

THE DANCE IS A FLASH IN TIME

Word-forsaker, motion-maker,
   rhythm-riding dancing girl!
Surging urge in leap or whirl
    joy-expending,
     life-commending,
taut and limber, limp and firm!
  Flung flesh in a blood-beat swirl!
  Spun-swivelled in looping line!
Body a hoop and a shaft and a loom
weaving a vanishing filigree form
    earth-transcending,
     time suspending!
      Soar!
      More—
The dance . . .
           is ending.

WITH DANCING FEET

Good metered verse can make words sing
   for it is true to all man's moods
     since he is rhythmic in his joy
   or grief, and in his lively feuds,
     the hot blood high, he will employ
impulsive movement that will bring

relief. It will be, stamp or sway,
   spondee, iamb, or anapest,
     for this began within the womb,
   continued at the mother's breast,
     a kicking, sucking, to the loom
of measured time. At work or play

all action moves with greatest ease
   when metronomic in its beat.
     Verse can be made in other ways,
   but is good meter obsolete?
     Why, it is not a passing phase
and we can spare our obsequities!

A verse must have a nice conceit
   and much depends on how it's done.
     Words will not always sing or dance
   no matter how a verse is spun
     and merit often seems pure chance—
But man was born with dancing feet!

TO A POET WHO BELITTLES
RHYME AND RHYTHM

Oh Menke dear, you're wrong, you're wrong!
There's rhythm in the sea-shaped shell
and heartbeat in the rampant rhyme.
Each flowering thing in its own time
will come, each bud will swell;
moon-tug of tide will bring the long
slow ebb and flow; in spring, bird song
will flood our fields; we can foretell
the hour of sunrise we call prime;
we watch the constellations climb;
Orion, rising, casts a spell
that silences the insect throng.
We're part of nature, we belong
within its rhythms that impel
a rhythm in ourselves. The grime
and crush of cities, and the slime
we make, and our atomic hell
will rouse no music, singing, strong,
to match what's inbred, of the heart
which is, I think, the source of art.

WORDS ARE FOR SHARING

You shall not read a line I write
and wonder what I could have meant!
Time spent will twine the sound with sense
without pretense to be profound
or erudite. My wish is not
to daze, astound, but to requite
what heed is lent to urgency
of song I know does not belong
to me alone. Oh no, I will not
write as though you were not there,
as though I did not care what sense
or sound within a line were true!
What comes to me is meant for you;
as bearer, sharer, we unite.

THE VILLANELLE
With apologies to W. E. Henley

A horrid thing's the villanelle!
It gives such trouble with its rhyme.
I know its teasing all too well!

It is enough to make one quell,
this forcing words so they will chime.
A horrid thing's the villanelle!

A luring little bagatelle
confounding poets in their prime—
I know its teasing all too well!

It suits a poet in a cell
with hours to spend, no count of time.
A horrid thing's the villanelle!

Then why do poets not rebel
but act like birds caught fast in lime?
I know its teasing all too well!

Because it's there. It casts that spell.
Ask why a mountain makes men climb.
A horrid thing's the villanelle!
I know its teasing all too well!

A USEFUL BEAST

Oh, poor Reason, how it labors!
A tired old horse that hauls its heavy load
of honest logic, not knowing where.
It butts its head on every paradox,
goes round, starts off again,
gallops for a bit, then slows, balks,
road blocked, impassable proposition.
Again detour, and now it trots
but comes to hilly country, it must slow
and trudge against steep argument . . .
At least it knows it is a horse and must obey
the whip of Will, the Ego's sharp giddap!
But do, please, put blinders on the beast
and do not let him see how, and quite close by,
without a try, Pegasus mounts the air with ease.

"O SWEET EVERLASTING VOICES—"

be still, be still! It is enough that I
should serve you through the day but not all night
as well! What can I do to pacify
your clamor when I can no longer write,
too wearied now to find the form to fit
your fantasies? Go where some poet lies
awake in longing for a word, a bit
of all you have to give, go tantalize
that man, and end your riot in my head.
It is high time, at dawn, I went to bed!

FOR KINDNESS SHOWN

Love given that asks nothing in return
must be so honored that no recompense
is made. It is a gift not meant to earn
reward, and what have I of affluence
that I could hope to match in even trade
so fine and rare a gift? Can I compute
my debt and cancel it, a payment made?
In joyfulness, I shall become the mute
recipient of your munificence,
enriched by knowing that such things can be
as human kindliness, an excellence
in man, a spendthrift love, as shown to me.
   And yet at least this thank you must be said
   because my heart rebels against my head.